NAVIGATING ADHD

A PARENT'S JOURNEY THROUGH SCHOOL CHALLENGES

STEVEN FITCH

First Edition

ISBN: 979-8-89379-827-2

Printed in USA

For Amy

"The family. We were a strange little band of characters trudging through life sharing diseases and toothpaste, coveting one another's desserts, hiding shampoo, borrowing money, locking each other out of our rooms, inflicting pain and kissing to heal it in the same instant, loving, laughing, defending, and trying to figure out the common thread that bound us all together."

-Emma Bombeck

INTRODUCTION

Welcome to a journey of understanding, empathy, and practical solutions. This book is not just a guide but a narrative designed to connect with you on a deeper level, making the challenges and triumphs of parenting children with ADHD relatable and insightful. Through the stories of two families—one with a 7-year-old girl named Emily and the other with an 11-year-old boy named Ethan—we aim to illustrate real-life scenarios that occur frequently in the lives of school-aged children with ADHD.

THE POWER OF NARRATIVE

Stories have a unique ability to resonate with us, allowing us to see our own experiences reflected in the lives of others. By presenting this book as a narrative, we hope to create a bond between you, the reader, and the characters. You will see their struggles, feel their frustrations, and celebrate their victories, all while gaining insights into managing similar situations with your own children.

This narrative approach helps to humanize the challenges of ADHD, moving beyond clinical descriptions and statistics to the real emotions and experiences that families face. We believe that by connecting with the characters, you will feel less alone in your journey and more empowered to implement the strategies discussed.

REAL STORIES, FICTIONALIZED ACCOUNTS

While the events and characters in this book are fictionalized, they are based on real events that happen all the time with school-aged kids. Emily and Ethan's experiences are drawn from countless stories shared by parents, teachers, and counselors who work with children with ADHD. The scenarios depicted here reflect the common challenges and situations that arise, providing a comprehensive look at the ADHD landscape in the school environment.

YOU'RE NOT ALONE

One of the most isolating aspects of parenting a child with ADHD can be the feeling that no one else truly understands what you're going through. This book is here to remind you that you are not alone. The struggles you face are shared by many, and there is a community of parents, educators, and professionals who are navigating the same path. Through the experiences of Emily and Ethan's families, you will find camaraderie and support.

PRACTICAL STRATEGIES AND SOLUTIONS

Each chapter presents a specific scenario that Emily or Ethan encounters at school, ranging from difficulties focusing in class to managing emotional outbursts. After the scenario is presented, you will find detailed conversations with a counselor specializing in ADHD, who provides practical strategies and solutions tailored to each situation. These strategies are designed to be actionable and effective, offering you tools that can be implemented in your own life.

In addition, the book includes conversations between the parents of the two families, Sarah and Jack (Emily's parents) and Rachel (Ethan's mother). These discussions offer further insights and tips, grounded in real-life experiences. By seeing how these parents communicate and support each other, you will gain ideas for building your own support network.

BUILDING UNDERSTANDING AND EMPATHY

Understanding ADHD is crucial for developing empathy and effective strategies. This book aims to deepen your understanding of ADHD, not just from a clinical perspective but from an emotional and practical one. By following Emily and Ethan's stories, you will see how ADHD impacts various aspects of their lives, from academic performance to social interactions, and how different strategies can make a significant difference.

HOW TO USE THIS BOOK

You can read this book in a linear fashion, following the progression of Emily and Ethan's stories, or you can jump to the chapters that address the specific challenges you are currently facing. Each chapter is designed to stand alone, providing complete insights and strategies for the particular scenario it covers.

ENCOURAGEMENT AND HOPE

Parenting a child with ADHD can be a challenging journey, but it is also one filled with opportunities for growth, understanding, and connection. Through the stories in this book, we hope to offer you encouragement and hope. The strategies discussed here are not quick fixes but steps towards building a supportive and effective environment for your child.

Remember, you are not alone. As you read about Emily and Ethan, we hope you find comfort in knowing that others are walking a similar path and that there are practical solutions and a supportive community available to help you along the way.

Thank you for embarking on this journey with us. We hope this book becomes a valuable resource and a source of inspiration as you navigate the challenges and celebrate the successes of raising a child with ADHD.

A JOURNEY THROUGH COMMON CHALLENGES

Here's a glimpse of the journey you'll take through the chapters of this book:

- Difficulty Focusing in Class
- Hyperactivity During Quiet Time
- Forgetting Homework
- Impulsive Behavior on the Playground
- Difficulty Following Instructions
- Struggles with Group Work
- Challenges with Transition
- Disorganization
- Struggles with Time Management
- Overwhelmed by Large Projects
- Positive Reinforcement and Rewards
- Documenting Your Journey
- Final Thoughts
- Worksheet Ideas
- My Own Path

MEET THE FAMILIES

In a quaint suburban neighborhood, two families have forged a bond through shared experiences, laughter, and challenges. Their stories intertwine in ways that reflect the everyday realities of parenting children with ADHD, offering insights and empathy to those walking a similar path. Let's meet these families and learn a bit about their backgrounds.

THE MITCHELL FAMILY

Emily Mitchell is a lively 7-year-old girl with an infectious smile and an insatiable curiosity. She loves to explore the world around her, often getting lost in her imaginative play. Emily's boundless energy and enthusiasm are her strengths, but they also present challenges, particularly in structured environments like school.

Sarah Mitchell, Emily's mother, is a dedicated nurse with a compassionate heart. She balances her demanding job with the responsibilities of parenting, often finding herself navigating the complexities of ADHD with patience and resilience. Sarah is committed to understanding her daughter's needs and finding effective strategies to support her.

Jack Mitchell, Emily's father, works as an engineer. His analytical mind and problem-solving skills are invaluable in addressing the practical aspects of ADHD management. Jack is the calm and steady presence in the family, always ready to support Sarah and Emily with his logical approach and unwavering love.

THE THOMPSON FAMILY

Ethan Thompson is an adventurous 11-year-old boy with a passion for science and technology. His inquisitive nature drives him to ask endless questions, and his creativity shines through in his numerous projects. However, Ethan's ADHD often leads to challenges with focus and impulsivity, especially in the school environment.

Rachel Thompson, Ethan's mother, is a high school teacher who understands the educational system from the inside out. She is an advocate for her son's needs, constantly striving to bridge the gap between his potential and the demands of the classroom. Rachel's background in education equips her with unique insights and strategies to support Ethan.

David Thompson, Ethan's father, is a software developer. His flexible work schedule allows him to be actively involved in Ethan's daily life. David's calm demeanor and problem-solving skills complement Rachel's approach, creating a balanced and supportive environment for Ethan.

BACKGROUND AND CHALLENGES

Both families live in a tight-knit community where neighbors know each other, and children play together in the local park. The Mitchells and the Thompsons met through a neighborhood association meeting and quickly discovered their shared experiences in raising children with ADHD. Their bond grew stronger as they navigated the ups and downs of parenting together, finding solace and strength in their mutual support.

EMILY'S STORY

Emily's journey with ADHD began when she started kindergarten. Her teachers noticed that she had difficulty sitting still, often getting up during lessons to explore the classroom. She struggled to follow multi-step instructions and frequently lost focus during group activities. Sarah and Jack were initially overwhelmed by the feedback from school, unsure of how to help their daughter succeed in a structured environment.

After consulting with a pediatrician and undergoing an evaluation, Emily was diagnosed with ADHD. This diagnosis brought a mix of relief and uncertainty for the Mitchells. They were relieved to have an explanation for Emily's behavior but unsure of the best way to support her. Sarah immersed herself in research, while Jack focused on creating a supportive home environment.

ETHAN'S STORY

Ethan's ADHD diagnosis came when he was in third grade. His teachers noted that he was bright and creative but often disrupted the class with his impulsive behavior. He struggled with transitions and frequently forgot to complete or turn in his homework. Rachel, with her background in education, recognized the signs of ADHD and pushed for a thorough evaluation.

The diagnosis confirmed Rachel's suspicions and provided a framework for understanding Ethan's behavior. Rachel and David worked together to implement strategies at home and collaborated closely with Ethan's teachers to create a supportive school environment. They faced challenges along the way, but their commitment to Ethan's success never wavered.

A SUPPORTIVE NETWORK

Central to both families' stories is the role of a dedicated counselor, Dr. Olivia Harris, who specializes in working with children with ADHD. Dr. Harris provides guidance, support, and practical strategies tailored to each child's unique needs. Her insights help the families navigate the complexities of ADHD, offering a source of expertise and reassurance.

Dr. Harris's office becomes a regular destination for both the Mitchells and the Thompsons. Her compassionate and knowledgeable approach fosters a sense of hope and empowerment in the parents. Through their sessions with Dr. Harris, Sarah, Jack, Rachel, and David learn to better understand their children's behaviors and implement effective strategies to support them.

BUILDING A COMMUNITY

The bond between the Mitchells and the Thompsons extends beyond their shared challenges. They become each other's confidants, sharing victories and setbacks, and offering encouragement and advice. Their friendship exemplifies the power of community and mutual support in navigating the journey of raising children with ADHD.

In this book, you will follow the stories of Emily and Ethan as they encounter various challenges at school and home. Each chapter will present a scenario, followed by detailed discussions with Dr. Harris and conversations between the parents. These narratives are designed to provide practical strategies, emotional support, and a sense of connection for families facing similar experiences.

As you read, remember that you are not alone. The experiences of Emily and Ethan, though fictionalized, are rooted in real-life events that many families encounter. Through their stories, we hope to offer you insights, strategies, and a sense of solidarity on your journey with ADHD.

CHAPTER 1

DIFFICULTY FOCUSING IN CLASS

Emily Mitchell sat at her small desk in Mrs. Bennett's first-grade classroom, her legs swinging restlessly back and forth. The classroom was alive with the sounds of pencils scratching on paper, the hum of whispered conversations, and the occasional outburst of laughter. Mrs. Bennett, a patient and experienced teacher, stood at the front of the room, reading aloud from a colorful storybook.

"Once upon a time, in a faraway land…" Mrs. Bennett's voice was calm and soothing, but Emily's mind was far from the story. She found herself staring out the window, watching the branches of the big oak tree swaying in the breeze. Her gaze drifted to the colorful posters on the walls, then to the clock ticking away the minutes until recess.

"Emily?" Mrs. Bennett's voice cut through her daydream. "Can you tell us what happened in the story so far?"

Emily snapped back to reality, her cheeks flushing as she realized she had no idea what Mrs. Bennett had just read. Her classmates turned to look at her, some with curious eyes, others with impatient sighs. She stammered, searching for an answer, but her mind was blank.

Seeing Emily's discomfort, Mrs. Bennett gave her a reassuring smile and moved on, but Emily couldn't shake the feeling of embarrassment. This wasn't the first time she had trouble focusing during class, and it wouldn't be the last. Despite her best efforts, her mind often wandered, leaving her feeling lost and frustrated.

Later that day, during recess, Emily sat alone on a bench, her usual energetic play replaced by a thoughtful frown. She watched her classmates playing tag and wished she could join them without the cloud of worry hanging over her.

After school, Mrs. Bennett decided to speak with Sarah, Emily's mother. As Sarah walked into the classroom to pick up Emily, Mrs. Bennett approached her with a warm smile.

"Hi, Sarah. Do you have a few minutes to chat about Emily?" Mrs. Bennett asked.

"Of course," Sarah replied, her face immediately reflecting concern. "Is everything okay?"

"Emily is a wonderful student—bright, creative, and full of energy," Mrs. Bennett began. "But I've noticed she has a hard time staying focused during lessons. She often seems distracted and struggles to follow along with the class."

Sarah sighed, a mixture of relief and worry on her face. “I’ve noticed the same thing at home. She gets distracted easily and has trouble completing tasks.”

“I understand,” Mrs. Bennett said empathetically. “I think it would be helpful for us to work together to find some strategies that might help Emily stay engaged. Have you considered speaking with a counselor who specializes in ADHD?”

Sarah nodded. “We’ve been seeing Dr. Harris. She’s been very helpful, but I think we need more strategies for the classroom.”

“I’m glad to hear that,” Mrs. Bennett said. “Maybe we can all sit down together—Dr. Harris, you, Jack, and myself—and come up with a plan to support Emily.”

A few days later, Sarah and Jack met with Dr. Olivia Harris at her cozy office. The walls were adorned with calming colors and inspirational quotes, and the atmosphere was welcoming. Dr. Harris greeted them with a warm smile and invited them to sit down.

“Thank you for coming in today,” Dr. Harris began. “I’ve been working with Emily for a while now, and I understand she’s having some difficulty focusing in class.”

“Yes,” Sarah said. “Mrs. Bennett mentioned it to us, and we’ve noticed it at home too. We want to find ways to help her stay more focused.”

“Absolutely,” Dr. Harris agreed. “ADHD can make it challenging for children to stay attentive, especially in a structured environment like a classroom. But there are several strategies we can try to help Emily.”

Dr. Harris pulled out a notepad and began outlining some ideas.

“First, we can implement some simple techniques to help Emily manage her attention. One effective method is to use visual aids. For example, a visual schedule can help Emily understand what to expect throughout the day. You can use pictures or symbols to represent different activities, which can help her transition from one task to the next more smoothly.

“Second, we can introduce the use of fidget tools. Sometimes, giving children with ADHD something small to fidget with can help them focus better. It might be a stress ball, a fidget spinner, or even a piece of putty. These tools can help manage their need for movement without being disruptive.

“Third, we can establish a signal between Emily and her teacher. This could be a discreet hand signal or a card that Emily can place on her desk to indicate when she’s struggling to focus. This allows Mrs. Bennett to give her a gentle reminder or provide some extra support without drawing too much attention.

“Lastly, incorporating short, frequent breaks can make a significant difference. Instead of expecting Emily to sit still for long periods, we can schedule short breaks where she can stand up, stretch, or move around. These breaks can help reset her attention and reduce restlessness."

Sarah and Jack listened intently, jotting down notes.

"These are great ideas," Sarah said. "We can definitely try the visual schedule at home too."

"Absolutely," Dr. Harris nodded. "Consistency between home and school can reinforce these strategies. I also suggest regular check-ins with Mrs. Bennett to discuss what's working and what might need adjusting."

That evening, Sarah and Jack invited Rachel over for dinner. Rachel was eager to hear how the meeting with Dr. Harris went.

"How did it go with Dr. Harris?" Rachel asked as they settled around the dining table.

"It was really helpful," Sarah replied. "We discussed several strategies to help Emily stay focused in class. We're going to start using a visual schedule and introduce some fidget tools."

"That sounds promising," Rachel said. "Ethan has been using a visual schedule for a while now, and it's made a big difference. He knows what to expect and transitions between tasks more smoothly."

Jack nodded. "We're also going to establish a signal between Emily and her teacher, and incorporate more breaks during the day."

"Those short breaks have been a lifesaver for Ethan," Rachel agreed. "Sometimes just a few minutes of moving around can help him refocus."

Sarah smiled, feeling a sense of relief and camaraderie. "It's good to know we're on the right track. How's Ethan been doing lately?"

Rachel shared a few recent challenges and victories, and they all brainstormed together, sharing tips and offering support. The conversation was filled with empathy and encouragement, a reminder that they were not alone in this journey.

By implementing these strategies, parents can help their children with ADHD manage their attention and focus better, both at home and in school. This collaborative approach between parents, teachers, and counselors creates a supportive environment where children can thrive.

Key Points to Implement at Home

- Create a visual schedule using pictures or symbols to represent different activities. This helps children understand and anticipate what comes next, making transitions smoother.

- Introduce fidget tools such as stress balls, fidget spinners, or putty to help manage the need for movement and improve focus.

- Establish a signal between your child and their teacher to indicate when they need help with focusing. This can be a hand signal or a card they can place on their desk.

- Schedule short breaks throughout the day to allow your child to stand up, stretch, and move around. This can help reset their attention and reduce restlessness.

- Ensure that strategies used at school are also implemented at home to reinforce routines and expectations.

- Maintain regular communication with your child's teacher to discuss the effectiveness of strategies and make adjustments as needed.

By implementing these strategies, parents can help their children with ADHD manage their attention and focus better, both at home and in school. This collaborative approach between parents, teachers, and counselors creates a supportive environment where children can thrive.

CHAPTER 2

HYPERACTIVITY DURING QUIET TIME

Ethan Thompson sat at a small table in the school library, surrounded by the soft hum of whispers and the occasional turning of pages. It was quiet reading time, and the librarian, Mrs. Green, had set aside a collection of interesting books for the students. Ethan, however, found it difficult to concentrate. His legs bounced under the table, and he drummed his fingers on the book cover.

Mrs. Green noticed Ethan's restlessness from across the room. She had seen similar behavior before in other children with ADHD. While most of the students were engrossed in their books, Ethan was fidgeting, his eyes darting around the room. He picked up his book, put it down, and then started tapping his pencil on the table.

As the session continued, Ethan's movements became more noticeable. He shifted in his seat, dropped his pencil, and then bent down to pick it up, accidentally bumping the table and causing a small disruption. Mrs. Green decided it was time to address her observations with Ethan's mother, Rachel, but she chose to do so through an email to ensure the message was communicated clearly and concisely.

That evening, Rachel received an email from Mrs. Green:

Subject: Observations During Library Quiet Time

Dear Mrs. Thompson,

I wanted to share some observations I made during today's quiet reading time in the library. Ethan seemed to have difficulty sitting still and focusing on his book. He appeared quite restless and was frequently fidgeting and moving around in his seat. This behavior was somewhat disruptive to the quiet environment we strive to maintain.

I thought it might be important to bring this to your attention.

Best regards,
Mrs. Green
School Librarian

Rachel sighed as she read the email, feeling a familiar mix of concern and determination. She knew that managing Ethan's hyperactivity required a coordinated effort, and this was another piece of the puzzle.

The next day, Rachel decided to reach out to Dr. Olivia Harris, the counselor who had been working with Ethan on managing his ADHD symptoms. They scheduled a meeting to discuss strategies that could help Ethan during quiet times, both in the library and in other settings.

When Rachel and Ethan met with Dr. Harris, the atmosphere was warm and supportive. Dr. Harris listened carefully as Rachel described the librarian's observations and Ethan's struggles with staying still during reading time.

“Ethan, it sounds like you have a lot of energy, especially during quiet times,” Dr. Harris began. “That’s completely okay. There are ways we can help you manage that energy so you can focus better and still enjoy your reading time.”

Dr. Harris pulled out her notepad and started outlining some strategies.

“First, we can try incorporating short, structured breaks. During these breaks, you can stand up, stretch, or walk around for a minute before returning to your seat. This can help you release some of that energy.”

Ethan nodded, intrigued by the idea.

“Second, we can use fidget tools. These are small items that you can quietly use at your desk, like a stress ball or a fidget spinner. They can help you stay focused without being disruptive.”

Rachel took notes, feeling hopeful about these new strategies.

“Third, we can practice mindfulness techniques. Simple breathing exercises can help you calm your mind and body, making it easier to sit still and concentrate.”

Over the next few weeks, Ethan and Rachel implemented these strategies at home and discussed them with Mrs. Green for use in the library. Ethan began to use short breaks, fidget tools, and mindfulness exercises to manage his energy.

One evening, as they were getting ready for dinner, Rachel received a text from Sarah. She read it aloud to Ethan.

“Sarah says Emily has been having a hard time sitting still during reading time at school. She wants to know if we have any tips.”

Ethan grinned. “We should tell her about the breaks and the fidget tools. They really helped me.”

Rachel smiled, proud of Ethan’s progress. “I’ll share our strategies with her. It’s great that we can help each other.”

Later, Rachel and Ethan shared their experiences with Sarah and Jack, discussing the strategies that had worked for Ethan.

“Emily has been so frustrated with sitting still,” Sarah said. “We’ll definitely try these ideas.”

Jack nodded in agreement. “It sounds like a great plan. Thanks for sharing.”

As the evening went on, the families enjoyed each other's company, sharing stories and offering support. The bond between them grew stronger, a testament to the power of community and mutual understanding.

Key Points to Implement at Home

- Short, Structured Breaks: Incorporate brief, regular breaks during quiet activities to allow your child to move around and release energy.

- Fidget Tools: Provide small, quiet fidget tools like stress balls or fidget spinners to help your child manage their energy and focus better.

- Mindfulness Techniques: Practice simple breathing exercises and mindfulness techniques to help your child calm their mind and body.

- Consistency: Ensure that strategies used at home are also supported at school. Consistency helps reinforce routines and expectations.

- Regular Check-Ins: Maintain communication with your child's teacher and school librarian to discuss progress and make adjustments as needed.

By implementing these strategies, parents can help their children with ADHD manage their hyperactivity more effectively, improving their ability to focus during quiet times. This collaborative approach between parents, teachers, and counselors creates a supportive environment where children can thrive.

CHAPTER 3

FORGETTING HOMEWORK

Rachel Thompson sat at the kitchen table, sorting through the mail. Amid the usual bills and advertisements, she found Ethan's progress report from school. She opened it eagerly, curious to see how her son was doing in his classes. As she scanned the report, her heart sank. Ethan's grades were lower than expected, particularly in subjects where she knew he could excel.

Rachel noticed a pattern in the teacher's comments. Several mentioned that Ethan frequently forgot to turn in his homework, despite his participation in class and understanding of the material. She sighed, feeling a mix of frustration and concern. Forgetting homework had been an ongoing issue, but seeing it impact his grades so significantly was disheartening.

When Ethan came home from school, Rachel decided to talk to him about the progress report.

"Hey, Ethan," she called as he dropped his backpack by the door. "Can we talk for a minute?"

Ethan walked over, sensing the seriousness in his mother's tone. "What's up, Mom?"

Rachel showed him the progress report. "I got your report card today. Your teachers mentioned that you've been forgetting to turn in your homework a lot. Do you know why that's happening?"

Ethan glanced at the report and then looked away, his cheeks flushing with embarrassment. "I don't know. I just forget sometimes. I do the homework, but then I leave it at home or lose it in my backpack."

Rachel nodded, trying to stay calm and supportive. "I know it's hard to keep track of everything, but we need to find a way to help you remember. It's important for your grades and for you to show your teachers what you know."

Ethan sighed, clearly frustrated. "I try, Mom. But there's so much to remember, and sometimes I just forget."

Rachel hugged him, feeling his frustration. "I know, sweetie. We're going to figure this out together. I'm going to talk to Dr. Harris and see what strategies we can use to help you."

A few days later, Rachel and Ethan met with Dr. Olivia Harris. The walls of her office were adorned with calming colors and inspirational quotes, creating a welcoming atmosphere. Dr. Harris greeted them warmly and invited them to sit down.

"Thank you for coming in today," Dr. Harris began. "Rachel, you mentioned that Ethan has been having trouble remembering to turn in his homework. Is that right?"

"Yes," Rachel replied. "His progress report showed that he's been forgetting a lot of his assignments, even though he's doing the work. It's affecting his grades."

Dr. Harris nodded thoughtfully. "Ethan, it sounds like you're doing your homework but having trouble keeping track of it. Is that correct?"

"Yeah," Ethan said, fidgeting slightly in his seat. "I do the work, but then I forget to bring it to school or it gets lost in my backpack."

"Okay," Dr. Harris said with a reassuring smile. "We can work on this. There are several strategies we can try to help you remember your homework and keep it organized."

Dr. Harris pulled out her notepad and began outlining some ideas.

"First, let's create a homework checklist. This will be a simple list that you use every evening to make sure you have everything you need for the next day. You can keep it in your backpack or on your desk at home."

Ethan nodded, looking interested. "That sounds like it could help."

“Second, we can set up a dedicated homework folder. This will be a special folder where you put all your completed assignments. That way, they won’t get lost in your backpack.”

Rachel jotted down notes, feeling hopeful about these strategies.

“Third, we can use technology to our advantage. We can set up reminders on your phone or a family calendar to remind you to pack your homework each night. Multiple reminders can reinforce the habit.”

Ethan smiled, feeling more confident. “I think that could really help. I’m always on my phone anyway.”

“Lastly,” Dr. Harris continued, “we can establish a routine where you pack your backpack at the same time every evening. Consistency is key to building a reliable habit.”

That evening, Rachel and Ethan sat down to create the homework checklist and set up the dedicated homework folder. They also programmed reminders into Ethan’s phone and discussed the new evening routine.

“Okay, Ethan,” Rachel said as they finished. “We’re going to do this together. Every evening, we’ll go through the checklist, make sure your homework is in the folder, and set your reminders. How does that sound?”

Ethan smiled, feeling hopeful. “It sounds good, Mom. I think this will help.”

The next day, Rachel shared the new strategies with Sarah and Jack when they came over for dinner. Sarah and Jack were eager to hear how the meeting with Dr. Harris went.

“How did it go with Dr. Harris?” Sarah asked as they settled around the dining table.

“It was really helpful,” Rachel replied. “We discussed several strategies to help Ethan remember his homework. We’re using a checklist, a dedicated homework folder, and setting reminders on his phone.”

“That sounds promising,” Jack said. “We’ve been having some similar issues with Emily. She often forgets her assignments too.”

Rachel nodded. “Consistency and routine seem to be key. We’re going to try and stick to the same process every evening.”

“That’s a great plan,” Sarah said. “We’ll definitely try these ideas with Emily.”

As the evening went on, the families enjoyed each other’s company, sharing stories and offering support. The bond between them grew stronger, a testament to the power of community and mutual understanding.

Key Points to Implement at Home

- Homework Checklist: Create a simple, reusable checklist to help your child remember their assignments. Use it every evening to ensure all homework is packed.

- Dedicated Homework Folder: Use a special folder to keep all completed assignments organized and prevent them from getting lost.

- Technology Reminders: Set up phone alarms, calendar alerts, or apps to remind your child to pack their homework. Multiple reminders can reinforce the habit.

- Consistent Routine: Establish a specific time each evening for your child to pack their backpack. Consistency helps build reliable habits.

- Regular Check-Ins: Maintain communication with your child's teacher to discuss progress and make adjustments as needed.

By implementing these strategies, parents can help their children with ADHD manage their homework more effectively, reducing stress and building confidence. This collaborative approach between parents, teachers, and counselors creates a supportive environment where children can thrive.

CHAPTER 4

IMPULSIVE BEHAVIOR ON THE PLAYGROUND

Ethan Thompson sprinted across the playground, his breath coming in short bursts as he chased after the soccer ball. The recess field was buzzing with the excitement of various games and activities, but Ethan's attention was solely focused on the ball. He loved playing soccer with his friends, feeling the rush of the game as he darted around, trying to score a goal.

Today, however, Ethan's energy seemed to be at an all-time high. As he closed in on the ball, he saw Ben, a classmate, also running towards it. Without thinking, Ethan impulsively shoved Ben out of the way to get to the ball first. Ben stumbled and fell, hitting the ground with a thud. The other kids stopped playing, their expressions shifting from excitement to shock.

"Hey, Ethan! What's your problem?" one of the kids shouted.

Ethan's heart sank as he realized what he had done. Ben got up, dusting himself off and glaring at Ethan.

“Why did you push me?” Ben demanded, his voice angry and hurt.

“I… I didn’t mean to,” Ethan stammered, feeling a wave of guilt wash over him.

Mrs. Johnson, the playground supervisor, quickly walked over to the scene. “What happened here?” she asked, looking from Ben to Ethan.

“Ethan pushed me,” Ben said, his eyes welling up with tears. “I wasn’t even doing anything!”

Mrs. Johnson sighed and looked at Ethan. “Ethan, we don’t push people. You know better than that. Come with me.”

Ethan followed Mrs. Johnson to the side of the playground, his head hanging low. He felt terrible about what had happened and worried about getting into trouble. As they sat on a bench, Mrs. Johnson called the school counselor, Dr. Peterson, to come and talk to Ethan.

A few minutes later, Dr. Peterson arrived, her calm presence immediately making Ethan feel a bit better.

“Hi, Ethan,” Dr. Peterson said kindly. “Can you tell me what happened?”

Ethan took a deep breath and explained how he had pushed Ben without thinking.

“I just wanted to get the ball,” Ethan said, his voice barely above a whisper. “I didn’t mean to hurt him.”

“I understand,” Dr. Peterson replied. “Sometimes our impulses can get the better of us, especially when we’re excited or focused on something. But it’s important to find ways to manage those impulses so we don’t hurt others.”

After talking with Ethan for a while, Dr. Peterson decided it would be helpful to involve Ethan’s mom, Rachel, in the conversation. She called Rachel and asked her to come to the school.

When Rachel arrived, she found Ethan sitting with Dr. Peterson, looking remorseful. She gave him a reassuring hug before sitting down to join the discussion.

“Thank you for coming, Rachel,” Dr. Peterson said. “Ethan and I were just talking about what happened on the playground today.”

Rachel nodded, concern etched on her face. “Ethan told me he had some trouble controlling his impulses. We’ve been working on it, but it’s been challenging.”

“That’s understandable,” Dr. Peterson replied. “ADHD can make impulse control particularly difficult. But there are strategies we can use to help Ethan manage his impulses better.”

Dr. Peterson outlined a few ideas.

“First, we can use role-playing to practice different scenarios where Ethan might feel impulsive. By acting out these situations, Ethan can learn to recognize the feeling of an impulse and practice making better choices.”

“Second, we can introduce a ‘stop-and-think’ technique. This involves teaching Ethan to pause and count to five before reacting. It gives him a moment to think about what he’s doing and make a more thoughtful decision.”

“Third, we can use positive reinforcement to encourage good behavior. When Ethan controls his impulses well, we can reward him with praise or a small reward. This helps reinforce the behavior we want to see.”

Rachel listened attentively, jotting down notes. “These sound like great strategies. We’ll definitely try them at home.”

“That’s great,” Dr. Peterson said. “Consistency is key. And Ethan, remember that it’s okay to make mistakes. What’s important is that you learn from them and keep trying.”

Ethan nodded, feeling a bit more hopeful. “I’ll try my best.”

That evening, Rachel and Ethan sat down to talk about what had happened.

“I know you didn’t mean to hurt Ben,” Rachel said gently. “But it’s important to think before you act. Let’s practice some of the strategies Dr. Peterson suggested.”

They spent some time role-playing different scenarios, with Rachel pretending to be another kid on the playground. They practiced the 'stop-and-think' technique, with Ethan pausing and counting to five before reacting.

Over the next few weeks, Ethan worked hard on controlling his impulses. He used the 'stop-and-think' technique regularly and found that it helped him make better decisions. Rachel praised him for his efforts, and they celebrated each small victory together.

One afternoon, as they were getting ready for dinner, Rachel received a text from Sarah. She read it aloud to Ethan.

"Sarah says Emily had some trouble with impulsive behavior at school today. She pushed another kid to get a toy. She wants to know if we have any tips."

Ethan grinned. "We should tell her about the 'stop-and-think' technique. It really helped me."

Rachel smiled, proud of Ethan's progress. "I'll share our strategies with her. It's great that we can help each other."

Later, Rachel and Ethan shared their experiences with Sarah and Jack, discussing the role-playing exercises and the 'stop-and-think' technique.

"Emily has been so upset about what happened," Sarah said. "We'll definitely try these ideas."

Jack nodded in agreement. “It sounds like a great plan. Thanks for sharing.”

As the evening went on, the families enjoyed each other’s company, sharing stories and offering support. The bond between them grew stronger, a testament to the power of community and mutual understanding.

Key Points to Implement at Home

- Role-Playing: Practice different scenarios where your child might feel impulsive. Role-playing helps them recognize the feeling of an impulse and practice making better choices.

- Stop-and-Think Technique: Teach your child to pause and count to five before reacting. This gives them a moment to think about what they’re doing and make a more thoughtful decision.

- Positive Reinforcement: Use praise or small rewards to encourage good behavior. Positive reinforcement helps reinforce the behavior you want to see.

- Consistency: Ensure that strategies used at home are also supported at school. Consistency helps reinforce routines and expectations.

- Regular Check-Ins: Maintain communication with your child’s teacher and school counselor to discuss progress and make adjustments as needed.

By implementing these strategies, parents can help their children with ADHD manage their impulses more effectively, reducing incidents of impulsive behavior and building confidence. This collaborative approach between parents, teachers, and counselors creates a supportive environment where children can thrive.

CHAPTER 5

DIFFICULTY FOLLOWING INSTRUCTIONS

Sarah Mitchell and Rachel Thompson met for lunch at their favorite café, taking a break from their busy schedules. They enjoyed these moments of catching up, sharing their experiences of parenting children with ADHD. Today, however, Sarah seemed particularly concerned.

As they settled into their seats and ordered their meals, Rachel noticed Sarah's pensive expression.

"What's on your mind, Sarah?" Rachel asked, sipping her iced tea.

Sarah sighed. "Emily has been having a really hard time following instructions in class, especially during science projects. Mrs. Bennett sent home a note saying that Emily often gets overwhelmed and doesn't complete the tasks correctly. It's affecting her confidence."

Rachel nodded sympathetically. "Ethan has had similar issues. He gets frustrated with multi-step instructions and sometimes gives up before finishing. It's tough to watch."

Sarah leaned in, her voice filled with concern. “Emily loves science, but she ends up in tears because she can’t keep up with the steps. It’s heartbreaking.”

Rachel reached across the table, giving Sarah’s hand a supportive squeeze. “It’s so hard to see them struggle with something they’re passionate about. Maybe we can talk to Dr. Harris together and find some strategies to help them.”

Sarah agreed. “That sounds like a good idea. I’ll set up a session with Dr. Harris.”

Later that week, Sarah and Jack met with Dr. Olivia Harris to discuss Emily’s difficulties with following multi-step instructions. Dr. Harris listened attentively as Sarah described Emily’s struggles in class.

“Thank you for sharing this with me,” Dr. Harris began. “It’s common for children with ADHD to have trouble with multi-step instructions, as they can easily become overwhelmed. But there are effective strategies we can use to help Emily.”

Dr. Harris pulled out her notepad and began outlining some ideas.

“First, we can use visual aids and written instructions. Providing Emily with a visual step-by-step guide for her tasks can help her follow along more easily. She can refer back to the guide as she completes each step.”

Sarah nodded, taking notes. “That makes sense. Emily is very visual, so that could really help her.”

“Second, we can teach Emily to break down tasks into smaller, more manageable parts,” Dr. Harris continued. “Instead of seeing the whole project as one big task, she can focus on one step at a time. This can reduce her anxiety and make the process more manageable.”

Jack looked thoughtful. “We can practice this at home too, with her chores or homework. It might help her get used to breaking tasks down.”

“Exactly,” Dr. Harris agreed. “Third, we can use verbal prompts and cues to guide Emily through the tasks. Gentle reminders from her teacher can help her stay on track without feeling rushed.”

Sarah smiled. “Mrs. Bennett is very supportive. I’m sure she’ll be willing to help with this.”

“Lastly, we can encourage Emily to ask for help when she feels stuck,” Dr. Harris said. “Letting her know that it’s okay to ask for assistance can reduce her anxiety and improve her confidence.”

A few days later, Sarah and Rachel met again, this time with their families, to share the strategies they had discussed with Dr. Harris.

“How did it go with Dr. Harris?” Rachel asked as they settled around the dining table.

"It was really helpful," Sarah replied. "We talked about using visual aids, breaking down tasks, and giving Emily verbal prompts. We're also encouraging her to ask for help when she needs it."

Rachel nodded. "Those sound like great strategies. Ethan responds well to visual aids too. We've been using a checklist for his homework, and it's made a big difference."

Jack added, "We're going to practice breaking tasks down at home with her chores and other activities. Consistency will be key."

As the evening went on, the families enjoyed each other's company, sharing stories and offering support. The bond between them grew stronger, a testament to the power of community and mutual understanding.

The next day, Sarah and Jack sat down with Emily to talk about the new strategies.

"Emily, we know you've been having a hard time with your science projects," Sarah began gently. "We've talked to Dr. Harris, and she suggested some ways to help you."

Emily looked up, her eyes wide with curiosity. "What are they?"

"We're going to use visual aids to help you follow the steps," Jack explained. "You'll have a step-by-step guide to look at while you work."

"And we're going to practice breaking tasks down into smaller parts," Sarah added. "This way, you can focus on one step at a time without getting overwhelmed."

Emily nodded, a small smile forming on her face. "That sounds like it could help."

"We also want you to know that it's okay to ask for help if you need it," Sarah said. "Mrs. Bennett and we are here to support you."

Over the next few weeks, Emily's parents and Mrs. Bennett implemented the new strategies. Emily started using visual step-by-step guides for her tasks, and they practiced breaking down complex instructions into smaller, more manageable steps. Mrs. Bennett also gave Emily gentle verbal prompts during class, helping her stay on track.

One afternoon, as they were getting ready for dinner, Sarah received a text from Mrs. Bennett. She read it aloud to Emily.

"Mrs. Bennett says you did a great job following the steps in today's science project," Sarah said, beaming with pride. "She said you used your visual guide and took your time with each step."

Emily grinned. "I really like the guide, Mom. It makes it so much easier to know what to do next."

Sarah hugged Emily, feeling proud of her progress. "I'm so proud of you, sweetheart. You're doing a fantastic job."

Later, Rachel and Ethan shared their experiences with Sarah and Jack, discussing the visual aids and the importance of breaking down tasks.

“Emily has been so much more confident with her tasks,” Sarah said. “The visual guide really helps her stay focused.”

Jack nodded in agreement. “It sounds like a great plan. Thanks for sharing.”

As the evening went on, the families enjoyed each other’s company, sharing stories and offering support. The bond between them grew stronger, a testament to the power of community and mutual understanding.

Key Points to Implement at Home

- Visual Aids: Use visual step-by-step guides to help your child follow multi-step instructions. This helps them refer back to the guide and stay on track.

- Break Down Tasks: Teach your child to break down complex tasks into smaller, more manageable parts. Focus on completing one step at a time.

- Verbal Prompts and Cues: Provide gentle reminders and verbal prompts to guide your child through tasks. This helps them stay focused and reduces the feeling of being rushed.

- Encourage Asking for Help: Let your child know it's okay to ask for help when they feel stuck. This can reduce anxiety and build confidence.

- Consistency: Ensure that strategies used at home are also supported at school. Consistency helps reinforce routines and expectations.

- Regular Check-Ins: Maintain communication with your child's teacher to discuss progress and make adjustments as needed.

By implementing these strategies, parents can help their children with ADHD manage multi-step tasks more effectively, reducing stress and building confidence. This collaborative approach between parents, teachers, and counselors creates a supportive environment where children can thrive.

CHAPTER 6

STRUGGLES WITH GROUP WORK

It was a sunny Saturday afternoon, and Ethan was at his classmate Ben's house, working on a group project for history class. The project was on ancient civilizations, and each member of the group had specific tasks to complete. Ethan was excited about the topic but found it hard to stay focused on his assigned part.

Ben's mom, Mrs. Carter, had generously offered to host the group. She provided snacks and set up a large table for the kids to spread out their materials. As the children worked, she noticed that Ethan seemed to dominate the conversation, often interrupting his peers and insisting on doing things his way.

"Why don't we focus on ancient Egypt?" Ethan suggested enthusiastically. "I can handle all the research on the pyramids and the pharaohs."

Ben nodded, but before he could respond, Ethan continued, "I've already got some great ideas. We can make a model of the pyramids, and I'll do the presentation."

Sophie, another classmate, tried to interject. “I think we should all share the work equally. Maybe we can each take a part of the presentation.”

Ethan frowned. “But I’ve got this great plan. It’ll be awesome if we do it my way.”

Mrs. Carter observed this interaction with growing concern. She noticed that the other kids were becoming frustrated, and Ethan’s dominant behavior was causing tension within the group. She decided it was important to share her observations with Rachel.

Later that evening, Mrs. Carter called Rachel. After some initial pleasantries, she gently brought up the topic.

“Rachel, I wanted to talk to you about something I noticed during the group project today,” Mrs. Carter began. “Ethan seems very enthusiastic, but he tends to dominate the conversation and struggles to listen to the other kids’ ideas. I thought it might be something you’d want to be aware of.”

Rachel sighed, a mix of concern and frustration washing over her. “Thank you for letting me know, Mrs. Carter. We’ve noticed similar behavior at home. He gets so excited and sometimes forgets to consider others.”

“I understand,” Mrs. Carter said kindly. “I just wanted to bring it to your attention. Maybe there are some strategies that could help him work better in a group setting.”

Rachel agreed. “I’ll definitely look into it. Thank you for letting me know.”

The next day, Rachel and Ethan met with Dr. Olivia Harris to discuss the issues Ethan was having with group work. Dr. Harris listened attentively as Rachel described the situation.

“Thank you for sharing this with me,” Dr. Harris began. “It’s not uncommon for children with ADHD to struggle with group dynamics. Their enthusiasm and desire to contribute can sometimes come across as dominating or not listening to others. Let’s discuss some strategies that might help Ethan.”

Dr. Harris pulled out her notepad and began outlining some ideas.

“First, we can introduce structured roles within the group. Each student can have a specific role, such as researcher, note-taker, or presenter. This helps clarify responsibilities and ensures that everyone has a chance to contribute.”

Ethan nodded, looking interested. “That sounds like it could help. Sometimes I don’t know what everyone else should do, so I just try to do it all.”

“Second, we can practice active listening skills,” Dr. Harris continued. “Ethan, you can learn to listen to your peers and acknowledge their ideas before sharing your own. We can use role-playing exercises to practice these skills.”

Rachel smiled. “That sounds like a good idea. We can practice that at home too.”

“Third,” Dr. Harris said, “we can use turn-taking techniques. For example, using a talking stick or setting a timer can ensure that everyone has an equal opportunity to speak and contribute during group activities.”

Ethan grinned. “I like the idea of a talking stick. It sounds fun and fair.”

“Lastly,” Dr. Harris added, “we can set clear group goals and expectations. Defining what needs to be accomplished and how the group will work together can help Ethan understand the importance of collaboration.”

Rachel and Ethan both felt hopeful as they left Dr. Harris’s office, armed with new strategies to try. Over the next few weeks, they practiced these techniques at home and discussed them with Ethan’s teacher, Mrs. Lewis, to implement them in the classroom as well.

One afternoon, as Rachel and Ethan were working on his homework, Rachel received a text from Sarah. She read it aloud to Ethan.

“Sarah says Emily had some trouble with her group project today. She kept interrupting her classmates and wanted to do everything herself. She wants to know if we have any tips.”

Ethan grinned. “We should tell her about the talking stick and the structured roles. They really helped me.”

Rachel smiled, proud of Ethan's progress. "I'll share our strategies with her. It's great that we can help each other."

Later, Rachel and Ethan shared their experiences with Sarah and Jack, discussing the structured roles and active listening practice.

"Emily has been so frustrated with group work," Sarah said. "We'll definitely try these ideas."

Jack nodded in agreement. "It sounds like a great plan. Thanks for sharing."

As the evening went on, the families enjoyed each other's company, sharing stories and offering support. The bond between them grew stronger, a testament to the power of community and mutual understanding.

Key Points to Implement at Home

- Structured Roles: Assign specific roles within group activities, such as researcher, note-taker, or presenter. This helps clarify responsibilities and ensures everyone has a chance to contribute.

- Active Listening Skills: Teach your child to listen to their peers and acknowledge their ideas before sharing their own. Use role-playing to practice these skills.

- Turn-Taking Techniques: Use a talking stick or set a timer to ensure everyone has an equal opportunity to speak and contribute during group activities.

- Clear Group Goals: Set clear group goals and expectations. Define what needs to be accomplished and how the group will work together to achieve these goals.

- Consistency: Ensure that strategies used at home are also supported at school. Consistency helps reinforce routines and expectations.

- Regular Check-Ins: Maintain communication with your child's teacher to discuss progress and make adjustments as needed.

By implementing these strategies, parents can help their children with ADHD manage group work more effectively, improving their ability to collaborate and reducing stress. This collaborative approach between parents, teachers, and counselors creates a supportive environment where children can thrive.

CHAPTER 7

CHALLENGES WITH TRANSITIONS

It was a typical Saturday morning at the Mitchell household. Emily was deeply engrossed in her art project, her face lit up with concentration as she carefully painted a colorful landscape. Sarah watched her daughter with a smile, admiring her dedication and creativity. The house was peaceful, filled with the quiet hum of productivity.

Suddenly, the tranquility was interrupted by the ringing of Sarah's phone. She picked it up, recognizing her mother's number.

"Hi, Mom. What's up?" Sarah said, her tone light.

"Sarah, we have a bit of an emergency here," her mother replied, sounding flustered. "We've got a water leak, and your father and I are having trouble handling it. Could you and Jack come over to help?"

Sarah's mind raced as she considered the request. "Of course, Mom. We'll be there as soon as we can."

She hung up and turned to Emily, who was still absorbed in her painting. "Emily, sweetie, we need to go to Grandma and Grandpa's house. They have a water leak, and they need our help."

Emily looked up, her face falling as she processed the sudden change. "But, Mom, I'm not finished with my painting. I can't leave now."

Sarah sighed, trying to remain patient. "I know, Emily, but this is important. We can come back and finish your painting later."

Emily's eyes filled with frustration and anxiety. "No, I want to stay and finish it now! I don't want to go!"

Jack entered the room, sensing the tension. "What's going on?"

Sarah explained the situation, her concern growing as Emily's distress became more apparent. "Emily, we really need to go. It's just for a little while."

Emily's face turned red, and she began to cry. "I can't just stop! I want to finish my painting!"

Sarah and Jack exchanged worried glances. They knew this was more than just a simple tantrum; it was a genuine struggle for Emily to transition from one activity to another, especially without any warning.

As they tried to calm Emily down, Sarah's mind flashed back to a conversation she had with Mrs. Bennett a few weeks ago.

Flashback:

Mrs. Bennett had called Sarah to discuss Emily's difficulties in the classroom.

"Hi, Mrs. Mitchell. I wanted to talk to you about Emily. She's been having some trouble with transitions between activities. She often gets very anxious and upset when it's time to move from one task to another."

Sarah had listened, feeling a pang of concern. "I've noticed that at home too. She gets really upset when we have to change plans suddenly."

Mrs. Bennett had offered some advice. "It might help to give her more warning before transitions and to use visual schedules to help her see what's coming next. Consistency can also make a big difference."

Back in the present, Sarah realized that this was exactly what Mrs. Bennett had been talking about. Emily's struggle to transition from her art project to helping at her grandparents' house was another example of the same issue.

"Jack, I think we need to try giving Emily more warning and using a visual schedule like Mrs. Bennett suggested," Sarah said softly.

Jack nodded. "Let's see if we can make this work."

Sarah turned back to Emily, who was still upset. "Emily, I understand this is hard for you. How about we set a timer for ten minutes so you can finish a part of your painting, and then we'll go to Grandma and Grandpa's? We can come back to it later."

Emily sniffled, considering the offer. "Okay, but I need to know we'll come back soon."

"We promise," Jack said gently. "Let's get ready to go after the timer goes off."

Sarah set the timer, and Emily returned to her painting, feeling slightly more in control. Once the timer rang, Emily reluctantly put down her brush but was calmer, knowing she had a chance to finish a part of her work.

A few days later, Sarah and Rachel met with Dr. Olivia Harris to discuss strategies for helping Emily with transitions. Dr. Harris listened carefully as Sarah described the incident.

"Thank you for sharing this with me," Dr. Harris began. "Transitions can be particularly challenging for children with ADHD. It's important to provide them with clear signals and enough time to prepare for changes. Let's discuss some strategies that might help Emily."

Dr. Harris pulled out her notepad and began outlining some ideas.

“First, using visual schedules can be very effective. By showing Emily what to expect throughout the day, she can mentally prepare for transitions. You can use pictures or symbols to represent different activities.”

Sarah nodded, taking notes. “Emily responds well to visuals. That could really help.”

“Second, giving her advance warning before a transition can make a big difference,” Dr. Harris continued. “For example, setting a timer for ten minutes before a change can help her get ready mentally and emotionally.”

Jack looked thoughtful. “We tried that with the timer, and it seemed to help a bit.”

“Third,” Dr. Harris said, “incorporating consistent routines can provide a sense of security. If she knows what to expect and when, it reduces anxiety about the unknown.”

Sarah smiled. “We’ll definitely work on establishing more consistent routines.”

“Lastly,” Dr. Harris added, “positive reinforcement for smooth transitions can encourage her to handle changes better. Praising her or offering a small reward when she transitions well can build her confidence.”

Over the next few weeks, Sarah and Jack implemented these strategies at home. They used a visual schedule to map out Emily’s day and gave her advance warnings before transitions. They also worked on creating consistent routines and praised Emily for successfully managing changes.

One afternoon, as they were getting ready for dinner, Sarah received a text from Rachel. She read it aloud to Jack.

"Rachel says Ethan had a hard time transitioning from recess to class today. He got really upset and didn't want to go back inside. She wants to know if we have any tips."

Jack smiled. "We should tell her about the visual schedule and the advance warnings. They've really helped Emily."

Sarah nodded. "I'll share our strategies with her. It's great that we can support each other."

Later, Sarah and Jack shared their experiences with Rachel and Ethan, discussing the visual schedules and the importance of giving advance warnings.

"Emily has been handling transitions so much better," Sarah said. "The visual schedule really helps her know what to expect."

Rachel nodded in agreement. "It sounds like a great plan. Thanks for sharing."

As the evening went on, the families enjoyed each other's company, sharing stories and offering support. The bond between them grew stronger, a testament to the power of community and mutual understanding.

Key Points to Implement at Home

- Visual Schedules: Use visual schedules to help your child see what activities are coming up next. This helps them prepare mentally for transitions.

- Advance Warning: Give your child advance warning before a transition. Setting a timer or providing verbal cues a few minutes before a change can help them get ready.

- Consistent Routines: Establish consistent routines to provide a sense of security. Knowing what to expect and when reduces anxiety about the unknown.

- Positive Reinforcement: Provide praise or small rewards for smooth transitions. This can encourage your child to handle changes better and build their confidence.

- Consistency: Ensure that strategies used at home are also supported at school. Consistency helps reinforce routines and expectations.

- Regular Check-Ins: Maintain communication with your child's teacher to discuss progress and make adjustments as needed.

By implementing these strategies, parents can help their children with ADHD manage transitions more effectively, reducing anxiety and building confidence. This collaborative approach between parents, teachers, and counselors creates a supportive environment where children can thrive.

CHAPTER 8

DISORGANIZATION

It was a typical Wednesday afternoon when Rachel received a call from the assistant principal, Mr. Hernandez. The sound of her phone ringing interrupted her thoughts as she prepared dinner. She answered, curious about the unexpected call.

“Hello, this is Rachel,” she said.

“Hi, Mrs. Thompson. This is Mr. Hernandez, the assistant principal at Ethan’s school. I hope I’m not catching you at a bad time,” he began.

“Not at all, Mr. Hernandez. Is everything okay with Ethan?” Rachel asked, her concern evident.

“Ethan is doing fine academically, but I wanted to talk to you about something I noticed today,” Mr. Hernandez said. “During recess, I saw Ethan’s backpack open, and it was quite a mess. Papers were crumpled, assignments were mixed with his lunchbox, and his supplies were scattered. It looked like he might be having some trouble staying organized.”

Rachel sighed, a mix of frustration and empathy washing over her. "We've been struggling with this at home too. He often loses track of his assignments and materials. It's been a real challenge."

Mr. Hernandez's tone softened. "I understand completely. As someone who has ADHD myself, I know how difficult it can be to stay organized. I've had to develop a lot of strategies over the years to manage it. I also know that you're working with Dr. Harris, who is fantastic. I thought I might offer some support and share a few strategies that helped me when I was in school."

Rachel's interest piqued. "That would be wonderful, Mr. Hernandez. Any help would be greatly appreciated."

"Great. How about we set up a meeting with you, Ethan, and Dr. Harris to discuss some strategies? I'm happy to be a part of it and share what I've learned," Mr. Hernandez suggested.

Rachel agreed, feeling a sense of relief and gratitude for the assistant principal's understanding and willingness to help. They scheduled a meeting for later that week.

When the day arrived, Rachel and Ethan met with Mr. Hernandez and Dr. Harris in the school's counseling office. Mr. Hernandez greeted them warmly and began the conversation.

"Thank you both for coming," Mr. Hernandez started. "Ethan, I know staying organized can be really tough. I struggled with it a lot when I was your age. But there are some things we can do to make it easier."

Ethan looked up, interested. "Like what?"

Dr. Harris smiled and jumped in. "Ethan, let's start with something simple. One effective strategy is to use a color-coded system. Each subject can have its own colored folder and notebook. This way, you can quickly see where everything belongs."

Rachel nodded, taking notes. "We can definitely set that up at home."

Mr. Hernandez added, "Another helpful tip is to use a daily planner. Writing down your assignments and checking them off as you complete them can keep you on track. It's a habit that takes time to build, but it's very effective."

Ethan looked thoughtful. "I think I can try that."

Dr. Harris continued, "We can also set up a routine for organizing your backpack every evening. Before you go to bed, take a few minutes to make sure everything is in its place for the next day. It helps reduce the morning rush and the chance of forgetting things."

Rachel smiled. "We'll start doing that. It's a good way to make sure we're prepared."

Mr. Hernandez nodded. "Consistency is key. It might be a bit tough at first, but once it becomes a habit, it will get easier. And remember, it's okay to ask for help. You're not alone in this."

Ethan felt a sense of reassurance from the conversation. "Thanks. I think this will really help."

Over the next few weeks, Rachel and Ethan implemented the new strategies at home. They set up a color-coded system for his school materials and started using a daily planner to keep track of assignments. Every evening, they went through Ethan's backpack together, making sure everything was in order for the next day.

One afternoon, as Rachel and Ethan were organizing his backpack, Rachel received a text from Sarah. She read it aloud to Ethan.

"Sarah says Emily's teacher mentioned her desk is always cluttered, and she's losing her assignments. She wants to know if we have any tips."

Ethan grinned. "We should tell her about the color-coded folders and the daily planner. They really helped me."

Rachel smiled, proud of Ethan's progress. "I'll share our strategies with her. It's great that we can help each other."

Later, Rachel and Ethan shared their experiences with Sarah and Jack, discussing the color-coded system and the evening routine.

“Emily has been so frustrated with losing her assignments,” Sarah said. “We’ll definitely try these ideas.”

Jack nodded in agreement. “It sounds like a great plan. Thanks for sharing.”

As the evening went on, the families enjoyed each other’s company, sharing stories and offering support. The bond between them grew stronger, a testament to the power of community and mutual understanding.

Key Points to Implement at Home

- Color-Coded System: Use color-coded folders and notebooks for each subject to help your child quickly see where everything belongs and stay organized.

- Daily Planner: Encourage your child to use a daily planner to write down assignments and check them off as they complete them. This helps keep track of tasks and deadlines.

- Evening Backpack Routine: Establish a routine for organizing your child’s backpack every evening. This helps reduce the morning rush and ensures everything is in its place for the next day.

- Consistency: Ensure that organizational strategies used at home are also supported at school. Consistency helps reinforce routines and expectations.

- Positive Reinforcement: Provide praise or small rewards for maintaining organization. This can motivate your child to keep up with the new habits.

- Regular Check-Ins: Maintain communication with your child's teacher to discuss progress and make adjustments as needed.

By implementing these strategies, parents can help their children with ADHD manage their organization more effectively, reducing stress and building confidence. This collaborative approach between parents, teachers, and counselors creates a supportive environment where children can thrive.

CHAPTER 9

STRUGGLES WITH TIME MANAGEMENT

Sarah Mitchell had recently started a new job in advertising, a role that required a lot of organization and time management. She was excited about the opportunity but also keenly aware of the challenges it brought. Her company had sent her to a conference on productivity and time management, and she eagerly attended, hoping to gather some tips and strategies that could help both her work and personal life.

The conference was held in a sleek, modern venue, filled with professionals eager to learn. As Sarah listened to the keynote speakers, she found herself relating many of the time management strategies to her own situation at home with Emily. The speakers talked about breaking down tasks, setting clear goals, using visual aids, and establishing routines—all concepts that could be beneficial for managing Emily's ADHD.

During one of the breakout sessions, the speaker discussed the Pomodoro Technique, a time management method that involves working in short, focused bursts with regular breaks.

Sarah's mind raced with ideas on how this could help Emily with her homework and daily tasks.

At the end of the conference, Sarah felt energized and inspired. She was eager to discuss what she had learned with Dr. Olivia Harris and explore how these strategies could be adapted for Emily.

A few days later, Sarah and Jack met with Dr. Harris in her office. The atmosphere was welcoming, as always, and Dr. Harris greeted them warmly.

"Thank you for coming in today," Dr. Harris began. "Sarah, you mentioned you attended a time management conference and had some ideas you wanted to discuss?"

"Yes," Sarah said, her voice filled with enthusiasm. "The conference was incredibly insightful. They talked about breaking down tasks, using visual aids, setting clear goals, and establishing routines. One technique that really stood out to me was the Pomodoro Technique. It involves working in short, focused bursts with regular breaks. I thought it might help Emily with her time management struggles."

Dr. Harris nodded, intrigued. "The Pomodoro Technique can be very effective, especially for children with ADHD. It helps maintain focus and makes tasks feel more manageable. Let's discuss how we can adapt these strategies for Emily."

Dr. Harris pulled out her notepad and began outlining some ideas.

“First, we can break down Emily’s tasks into smaller, more manageable parts,” Dr. Harris suggested. “Instead of seeing her homework as one big task, we can divide it into smaller segments. Each segment can be a ‘Pomodoro’ session, where she works for 25 minutes and then takes a 5-minute break.”

Jack looked thoughtful. “We can use a timer for this at home. It might help Emily feel less overwhelmed.”

Sarah nodded. “I also liked the idea of using visual aids. We could create a visual schedule for her, showing her tasks and break times. This way, she can see what she needs to do and when she’ll get a break.”

“Visual schedules are very effective,” Dr. Harris agreed. “They provide a clear structure and help children understand what to expect. We can also set clear goals for each session, so Emily knows what she needs to accomplish.”

“We’ll start by setting up a daily routine,” Sarah said. “We can incorporate the Pomodoro sessions into her homework time and other tasks. Consistency will be key.”

Dr. Harris smiled. “It sounds like a solid plan. Positive reinforcement can also be helpful. Praising Emily for staying on task and completing her sessions can motivate her to keep up with the new routine.”

Over the next few weeks, Sarah and Jack implemented the new strategies at home. They set up a visual schedule for Emily, breaking down her tasks into smaller segments and using the Pomodoro Technique. Emily's timer became an essential tool, helping her manage her time and stay focused.

One afternoon, as they were getting ready for dinner, Sarah received a text from Rachel. She read it aloud to Jack.

"Rachel says Ethan has been having a hard time managing his time with his science project. He keeps getting distracted and can't seem to finish his work. She wants to know if we have any tips."

Jack smiled. "We should tell her about the Pomodoro Technique and the visual schedule. They've really helped Emily."

Sarah nodded. "I'll share our strategies with her. It's great that we can support each other."

Later, Sarah and Jack shared their experiences with Rachel and Ethan, discussing the Pomodoro Technique and the importance of visual schedules.

"Emily has been so much more productive and less stressed," Sarah said. "The visual schedule and short, focused work sessions really help her stay on track."

Rachel nodded in agreement. "It sounds like a great plan. Thanks for sharing."

As the evening went on, the families enjoyed each other's company, sharing stories and offering support. The bond between them grew stronger, a testament to the power of community and mutual understanding.

Key Points to Implement at Home

- Pomodoro Technique: Use the Pomodoro Technique to help your child manage their time. Break tasks into 25-minute work sessions followed by 5-minute breaks. Use a timer to keep track.

- Visual Schedules: Create a visual schedule to help your child see their tasks and break times. This provides structure and helps them understand what to expect.

- Break Down Tasks: Divide larger tasks into smaller, more manageable parts. This makes them feel less overwhelming and more achievable.

- Set Clear Goals: Establish clear goals for each work session so your child knows what they need to accomplish.

- Consistent Routine: Establish a consistent daily routine incorporating the Pomodoro sessions. Consistency helps reinforce good habits.

- Positive Reinforcement: Provide praise and small rewards for staying on task and completing sessions. This can motivate your child to keep up with the new routine.

- Regular Check-Ins: Maintain communication with your child's teacher to discuss progress and make adjustments as needed.

By implementing these strategies, parents can help their children with ADHD manage their time more effectively, reducing stress and improving productivity. This collaborative approach between parents, teachers, and counselors creates a supportive environment where children can thrive.

CHAPTER 10

OVERWHELMED BY LARGE PROJECTS

Sarah Mitchell sat in the school library, surrounded by other parents who had come to attend an after-school workshop. The workshop was organized by Mrs. Bennett, Emily's history teacher, to explain the details of a six-week-long history project the students would be working on. The room was filled with a low hum of conversations as parents settled into their seats.

Mrs. Bennett stood at the front of the room, smiling warmly. "Thank you all for coming. Today, I'll be going over the details of the history project your children will be working on over the next six weeks. This project is designed to help them learn about different historical events and figures, and it will require both research and creativity."

Sarah listened attentively as Mrs. Bennett explained the project. The students would be required to choose a historical figure, conduct research, create a timeline, write a report, and prepare a presentation. It was a comprehensive project that would require careful planning and consistent effort.

After the presentation, Mrs. Bennett opened the floor for questions. Sarah raised her hand, feeling a mix of concern and determination.

"Mrs. Bennett, I've noticed that Emily often feels overwhelmed by large projects and assignments," Sarah began. "We've had several conversations about her progress this year, and I'm worried about how she'll handle such a long-term project. Do you have any suggestions on how I can help her stay on track and manage her workload effectively?"

Mrs. Bennett nodded, understanding the concern. "That's a great question, Sarah. It's important to break down large projects into smaller, more manageable tasks. This can help reduce the feeling of being overwhelmed. Let's discuss some strategies that can help Emily stay organized and focused."

After the workshop, Mrs. Bennett took some time to speak with Sarah one-on-one to offer more personalized advice.

"First," Mrs. Bennett suggested, "we can create a project timeline. Break down the entire project into weekly tasks. For example, the first week could be dedicated to choosing a historical figure and gathering initial research. The second week could focus on creating the timeline, and so on. This way, Emily can tackle the project step-by-step rather than feeling overwhelmed by the entire task."

Sarah nodded, taking notes. "That sounds like a great idea. We can use a calendar to mark each milestone."

"Exactly," Mrs. Bennett agreed. "Using visual aids like calendars or checklists can help Emily see her progress and stay motivated. It's also helpful to set specific goals for each work session. Instead of saying, 'Work on your project,' it can be more effective to say, 'Complete the introduction paragraph for your report.'"

Sarah smiled. "I think that will really help. Emily responds well to clear, specific instructions."

"Another strategy is to incorporate regular check-ins," Mrs. Bennett continued. "We can set up a schedule for Emily to meet with me every week to review her progress. This way, she can get feedback and adjust her plans if needed."

"That sounds reassuring," Sarah said. "Knowing that she has regular support from you will definitely help her stay on track."

"Lastly, don't forget to celebrate the small victories," Mrs. Bennett added. "Acknowledging her progress, even if it's just completing a small part of the project, can boost her confidence and keep her motivated."

Sarah felt more confident as she left the workshop, armed with strategies to help Emily manage her history project. She decided to discuss these ideas with Dr. Harris to get additional insights on how to support Emily.

A few days later, Sarah and Emily met with Dr. Olivia Harris. Dr. Harris listened carefully as Sarah described the history project and the strategies Mrs. Bennett had suggested.

“Thank you for sharing this with me, Sarah,” Dr. Harris began. “It sounds like Mrs. Bennett has provided some excellent strategies. Let’s build on those and tailor them specifically for Emily’s needs.”

Dr. Harris pulled out her notepad and began outlining additional ideas.

“First, we can use a visual project planner,” Dr. Harris suggested. “This can be a large poster or a digital app where Emily can see all the tasks laid out visually. Each task can be marked with a deadline, and she can check them off as she completes them. This helps provide a clear sense of progress.”

Sarah nodded, taking notes. “Emily loves visual tools. I think this will work well for her.”

“Second, let’s set up a reward system,” Dr. Harris continued. “For each milestone she completes, she can earn a small reward. This can be something she enjoys, like extra screen time or a special treat. Rewards can provide additional motivation.”

Emily smiled at the idea. “I like the sound of that!”

“Third, we can incorporate short, regular breaks during her work sessions,” Dr. Harris said. “Working in focused bursts with breaks in between can help maintain her concentration and prevent burnout.”

Sarah agreed. "We'll make sure to schedule regular breaks."

"Lastly," Dr. Harris added, "we can use mindfulness techniques to help Emily manage any anxiety she might feel about the project. Simple breathing exercises or short mindfulness practices can help her stay calm and focused."

Over the next few weeks, Sarah and Emily implemented the new strategies. They created a visual project planner and used a calendar to mark each milestone. Emily set specific goals for each work session and enjoyed earning small rewards for her progress. Regular check-ins with Mrs. Bennett provided her with the support and feedback she needed.

One afternoon, as they were working on the project, Sarah received a text from Rachel. She read it aloud to Emily.

"Rachel says Ethan is feeling overwhelmed by his science project. He's not sure how to start and keeps putting it off. She wants to know if we have any tips."

Emily grinned. "We should tell her about the project planner and the weekly check-ins. They really helped me."

Sarah smiled, proud of Emily's progress. "I'll share our strategies with her. It's great that we can help each other."

Later, Sarah and Emily shared their experiences with Rachel and Ethan, discussing the visual project planner and the importance of breaking down tasks.

"Emily has been so much more organized and less stressed," Sarah said. "The visual planner and specific goals really help her stay on track."

Rachel nodded in agreement. "It sounds like a great plan. Thanks for sharing."

As the evening went on, the families enjoyed each other's company, sharing stories and offering support. The bond between them grew stronger, a testament to the power of community and mutual understanding.

Key Points to Implement at Home

- Project Timeline: Break down large projects into smaller, manageable tasks and create a timeline to track progress. Use a calendar to mark each milestone.

- Visual Project Planner: Use a visual planner, either a poster or a digital app, to help your child see all the tasks laid out. Check off tasks as they are completed to provide a sense of progress.

- Specific Goals: Set clear, specific goals for each work session. This helps your child focus on one task at a time and reduces feelings of being overwhelmed.

- Regular Check-Ins: Schedule regular check-ins with the teacher or a counselor to review progress and provide feedback. This support helps keep your child on track.

- Reward System: Implement a reward system for completing milestones. Small rewards can provide additional motivation and encourage your child to stay on task.

- Regular Breaks: Incorporate short, regular breaks during work sessions to maintain concentration and prevent burnout.

- Mindfulness Techniques: Use simple breathing exercises or mindfulness practices to help your child manage anxiety and stay calm.

By implementing these strategies, parents can help their children with ADHD manage large projects more effectively, reducing stress and building confidence. This collaborative approach between parents, teachers, and counselors creates a supportive environment where children can thrive.

CHAPTER 11

POSITIVE REINFORCEMENT AND REWARDS

It was a warm Friday evening when the Mitchell and Thompson families decided to have dinner together at their favorite local restaurant. The cozy atmosphere of the restaurant buzzed with the sound of clinking cutlery and cheerful conversations. Sarah and Rachel had been discussing their children's progress and decided it was the perfect time to share the system they had developed to support their children's growth and behavior.

As they settled into their seats, the adults exchanged warm smiles, and the children eagerly picked up their menus. The server took their orders, and soon, the conversation turned to the topic at hand.

"Rachel and I have been talking a lot about how to take everything we've learned from our experiences and create a system that supports Ethan and Emily in all areas of their lives," Sarah began, her voice filled with enthusiasm. "We've come up with something we think could really help."

Rachel nodded, pulling out a notepad. “We’ve put together a structured plan that encompasses school grades, school behavior, at-home behavior, chores, and family interactions. We want to make sure Ethan and Emily have clear expectations and positive reinforcement to guide them.”

Jack looked intrigued. “That sounds like a great idea. How does it work?”

“First, we created a reward chart that covers different areas,” Rachel explained. “School grades, school behavior, at-home behavior, and chores all have specific goals and rewards associated with them. The idea is to give Ethan and Emily consistent, positive reinforcement for meeting their goals.”

Sarah continued, “For school grades, we set achievable targets based on their current performance. When they meet or exceed these targets, they earn points. The same goes for school behavior. We talked to their teachers to understand the key areas they need to work on, like paying attention in class, completing assignments on time, and cooperating with peers.”

Rachel added, “At home, we set goals for behavior and chores. For example, keeping their rooms tidy, helping set the table, and being respectful to family members. Each task and behavior has a point value, and they can earn points for completing them.”

Jack smiled, liking the idea. “What about family interactions?”

Sarah nodded. "We included family interactions to encourage positive relationships. For instance, spending quality time together without arguments, participating in family activities, and showing kindness to each other. These also earn points."

Ethan and Emily listened intently, their curiosity piqued. Emily looked up at her mother. "What do we do with the points?"

Rachel smiled at her daughter. "Good question, Emily. The points can be exchanged for rewards. We made a list of rewards you both can choose from, like extra screen time, a special outing, or a new book or toy. The more points you earn, the bigger the reward."

Jack nodded approvingly. "That sounds like a great way to motivate them and teach responsibility. How do we track their progress?"

"We created a chart that we'll keep in a common area at home," Sarah explained. "Each week, we'll sit down as a family to review the chart and see how many points Ethan and Emily have earned. It's a way to celebrate their successes and discuss any areas they need to work on."

Rachel added, "We also decided to include a section for reflections. Each week, Ethan and Emily will write down what they think went well and what they want to improve on. It's a way to help them become more self-aware and involved in their own growth."

As their meals arrived, the conversation continued with excitement and positivity. The children were eager to start earning points and working towards their rewards. The parents felt a sense of accomplishment, knowing they had created a system that would support their children's development in a comprehensive and balanced way.

Later that evening, as the families finished their dinner and prepared to leave, Sarah and Rachel exchanged knowing glances. They were proud of the progress their children had made and hopeful for the future.

Ethan looked up at his mother as they walked to the car. "Mom, I'm really excited about the reward chart. I think it's going to help me do better in school and at home."

Rachel smiled, hugging her son. "I'm excited too, Ethan. I know you're going to do great. We're all here to support you."

Emily chimed in, "I can't wait to start earning points! I'm going to try my best every day."

Sarah smiled at her daughter. "That's the spirit, Emily. We're so proud of you."

As the families drove home, they felt a renewed sense of hope and determination. The journey had been challenging, but they had learned so much along the way. With their new system in place, they were ready to support their children in becoming the best versions of themselves.

Key Points to Implement at Home

- Reward Chart: Create a reward chart that covers school grades, school behavior, at-home behavior, chores, and family interactions. Assign specific goals and point values for each area.

- Positive Reinforcement: Use points as positive reinforcement for meeting goals. Points can be exchanged for rewards like extra screen time, special outings, or new toys.

- Weekly Reviews: Hold weekly family meetings to review the reward chart, celebrate successes, and discuss areas for improvement. Use this time for reflections to help children become more self-aware.

- Consistency: Ensure consistency in expectations and reinforcement. Regularly update the chart and maintain clear communication about goals and rewards.

- Involvement: Involve children in the process by allowing them to choose some of the rewards and encouraging them to reflect on their progress and set personal goals.

By implementing this comprehensive system, parents can support their children with ADHD in all areas of their lives, fostering responsibility, self-awareness, and positive behavior. This approach creates a supportive and structured environment where children can thrive and feel motivated to succeed.

CHAPTER 12

DOCUMENTING YOUR JOURNEY

As a parent of a child with ADHD, it's essential to keep track of the steps you take to help your child manage their condition. Documenting both the successes and failures of your efforts is crucial for several reasons. It allows you to identify what strategies work best, recognize patterns in behavior, and adjust your approach as needed. Moreover, it provides valuable insights that can be shared with teachers, counselors, and healthcare providers to ensure a cohesive and supportive environment for your child.

Why Documenting Matters

1. Identifying Effective Strategies: Not every strategy will work for every child. By documenting your approaches and their outcomes, you can identify which methods are most effective in helping your child. This information can guide you in making informed decisions about future interventions.

2. Recognizing Patterns: Keeping detailed records helps you spot patterns in your child's behavior. You might notice that certain times of day, types of activities, or environmental factors influence your child's behavior and ability to focus.

Understanding these patterns allows you to tailor your strategies to better meet your child's needs.

3. Adjusting Approaches: Documenting both successes and failures enables you to adjust your strategies based on what works and what doesn't. This flexibility is crucial in managing ADHD, as what works today might not work tomorrow. Continuous documentation ensures that you can pivot quickly and effectively.

4. Communicating with Professionals: Sharing detailed records with teachers, counselors, and healthcare providers gives them a clearer picture of your child's progress and challenges. This collaborative approach ensures that everyone involved in your child's care is on the same page and can work together to support your child.

5. Empowering Your Child: As your child grows older, sharing documented successes and challenges with them can help them understand their condition better. It empowers them to take an active role in managing their ADHD, fostering self-awareness and responsibility.

How to Document Effectively

1. Daily Journals: Keep a daily journal where you note down your child's behavior, the strategies you used, and their outcomes. Include details such as the time of day, the setting, and your child's mood.

2. Weekly Summaries: At the end of each week, write a summary of the key observations. Highlight significant

successes and failures, and reflect on what might have contributed to these outcomes.

3. Monthly Reviews: Conduct a more comprehensive review at the end of each month. Look for patterns and trends that have emerged over the past weeks. Adjust your strategies based on these insights.

4. Use Technology: Consider using apps or digital tools designed for tracking behavior and interventions. These tools often come with features that allow you to generate reports and analyze data more effectively.

5. Include Your Child: Involve your child in the documentation process. Encourage them to express how they felt about the strategies used and what they think worked or didn't work. This can provide valuable insights from their perspective.

Journaling Questions to Track Progress

To help you document your journey effectively, here are 50 journaling questions you can use to track how you and your child are doing:

1. What strategies did I use today to help my child manage their ADHD?
2. How did my child respond to these strategies?
3. What time of day did I notice the most challenges?
4. What environmental factors seemed to influence my child's behavior?
5. Did my child complete their homework on time today?

6. How did my child handle transitions between activities?
7. What rewards or incentives seemed to motivate my child today?
8. Were there any significant successes today? If so, what were they?
9. What challenges did my child face today?
10. How did I address these challenges?
11. Did my child express any feelings of frustration or anxiety?
12. How did I help my child manage these feelings?
13. What physical activities did my child engage in today?
14. How did these activities impact their behavior?
15. What changes did I notice in my child's behavior at different times of the day?
16. How did my child's diet affect their behavior today?
17. Were there any social interactions that impacted my child's behavior?
18. How did I support my child during these interactions?
19. Did my child use any mindfulness or relaxation techniques today?
20. How effective were these techniques?
21. What academic tasks did my child struggle with today?
22. How did I help them overcome these struggles?
23. Did my child follow their visual schedule today?
24. How did following the schedule impact their behavior?
25. What feedback did I receive from my child's teacher today?
26. How did I incorporate this feedback into our strategy?
27. Did my child meet their behavior goals for the day?
28. How did we celebrate their successes?
29. What failures did we encounter today?
30. What can we learn from these failures?

31. How did I feel about my parenting today?
32. What could I do differently tomorrow?
33. How did my child feel about their progress today?
34. What goals can we set for tomorrow?
35. How did I involve my child in the planning process today?
36. Did my child show any signs of improvement in their behavior?
37. What contributed to these improvements?
38. How did our family's routine impact my child's behavior?
39. What adjustments can we make to improve our routine?
40. Did my child express any new interests today?
41. How can we incorporate these interests into their routine?
42. What was the most challenging part of the day?
43. How did I handle this challenge?
44. Did my child express gratitude or positive feelings today?
45. How did this make me feel?
46. What strategies can we try tomorrow to address today's challenges?
47. How can we build on today's successes?
48. What support do I need to help my child more effectively?
49. How can I better communicate with my child's teacher or counselor?
50. What positive changes have I noticed in my child's behavior over the past week?

By regularly documenting your experiences and reflecting on these questions, you can create a detailed record of your child's progress. This practice will not only help you identify effective strategies but also provide a valuable resource for everyone involved in supporting your child's journey with ADHD.

FINAL THOUGHTS

Building a Supportive Network for Children with ADHD

The journey of parenting a child with ADHD is a continuous process of learning, adapting, and growing. As Sarah and Rachel sat together at the local restaurant, discussing their experiences and the comprehensive system they had developed, they felt a sense of accomplishment and hope. Their journey was a testament to the power of community, understanding, and unwavering support.

Reflecting on the Journey

Sarah and Rachel had come a long way from the early days of confusion and frustration. They had faced numerous challenges and had to navigate the complexities of ADHD with patience and perseverance. They learned that no single strategy works for every child and that flexibility and adaptability are crucial. Through their experiences, they developed a deep understanding of their children's needs and how to address them effectively.

The system they created—encompassing school grades, school behavior, at-home behavior, chores, and family interactions—was a culmination of their efforts. It was designed to provide structure, consistency, and positive reinforcement, all of which are essential for children with

ADHD. This system not only helped their children manage their symptoms but also empowered them to take an active role in their own growth and development.

The Importance of Documentation

One of the key elements of their approach was the importance of documenting both successes and failures. Keeping detailed records allowed Sarah and Rachel to identify patterns, adjust strategies, and make informed decisions. It also provided valuable insights that could be shared with teachers, counselors, and healthcare providers, ensuring a cohesive and supportive environment for their children.

Documenting the journey also served as a reflective tool. By regularly reviewing their notes and journaling responses, Sarah and Rachel were able to see the progress their children were making. It gave them a sense of accomplishment and reinforced the idea that they were on the right path. Moreover, involving their children in the documentation process helped Ethan and Emily become more self-aware and responsible for their actions.

Creating a Supportive Environment

The comprehensive system they developed was grounded in creating a supportive environment that addressed various aspects of their children's lives. Here’s how each component of the system contributed to the overall well-being of Ethan and Emily:

1. School Grades: Setting achievable targets for school grades provided clear academic goals for the children. It motivated them to strive for improvement and gave them a sense of accomplishment when they met or exceeded these targets. By regularly reviewing their progress, Sarah and Rachel were able to provide timely support and encouragement.

2. School Behavior: Collaborating with teachers to identify key areas for improvement in school behavior helped Ethan and Emily develop better social skills and classroom etiquette. Positive reinforcement for good behavior encouraged them to consistently make better choices.

3. At-Home Behavior: Establishing clear expectations for at-home behavior created a structured environment where Ethan and Emily knew what was expected of them. This consistency helped reduce anxiety and provided a sense of stability.

4. Chores and Responsibilities: Assigning age-appropriate chores and responsibilities taught the children the importance of contributing to the household. It fostered a sense of responsibility and helped them develop time management and organizational skills.

5. Family Interactions: Emphasizing positive family interactions encouraged open communication, mutual respect, and empathy. Family activities and quality time strengthened their bond and provided a supportive network for both the children and parents.

Strategies for Success

Throughout their journey, Sarah and Rachel learned that successful strategies often involved a combination of approaches tailored to their children's unique needs. Here are some key strategies that proved effective:

1. Visual Aids and Schedules: Using visual aids, such as charts and calendars, helped Ethan and Emily understand their daily routines and upcoming tasks. Visual schedules provided a clear structure and helped them transition smoothly between activities.

2. Positive Reinforcement: Rewarding positive behavior and achievements with points that could be exchanged for rewards motivated the children to strive for success. It also helped them associate positive behavior with tangible benefits.

3. Consistent Routines: Establishing consistent routines for homework, chores, and bedtime provided a sense of predictability and security. Consistency in routines helped the children develop good habits and reduced the likelihood of behavioral issues.

4. Breaks and Mindfulness Techniques: Incorporating regular breaks during tasks and teaching mindfulness techniques helped the children manage their energy levels and stay focused. Techniques such as deep breathing and short relaxation exercises proved effective in reducing anxiety and improving concentration.

5. Regular Check-Ins: Scheduling regular check-ins with teachers and counselors ensured that everyone involved in the children's care was on the same page. These check-ins provided valuable feedback and allowed for timely adjustments to strategies.

Supporting Each Other as Parents

One of the most significant aspects of Sarah and Rachel's journey was the support they provided each other. Parenting a child with ADHD can be isolating and overwhelming, but having a supportive network made a tremendous difference. Here are some ways they supported each other:

1. Sharing Experiences: Regularly meeting to share their experiences, challenges, and successes provided a sense of camaraderie and understanding. They realized that they were not alone in their struggles and that they could learn from each other's experiences.

2. Collaborative Problem-Solving: When faced with challenges, Sarah and Rachel worked together to brainstorm solutions. This collaborative approach allowed them to come up with creative strategies that they might not have considered on their own.

3. Emotional Support: Providing emotional support during tough times helped them stay resilient. Whether it was a reassuring conversation after a difficult day or celebrating small victories together, their mutual support strengthened their resolve.

4. Resource Sharing: Sharing resources, such as books, articles, and contacts for professionals, enriched their knowledge and provided new perspectives. This exchange of information helped them stay informed and make better decisions for their children.

5. Encouragement and Validation: Encouraging each other and validating their feelings as parents of children with ADHD helped them maintain a positive outlook. Recognizing the efforts and progress of each other's children reinforced the idea that they were on the right path.

Looking Forward: Building a Brighter Future

As Sarah and Rachel reflected on their journey, they felt optimistic about the future. They had developed a system that worked for their families and had built a strong support network. They knew that the journey would continue to have its challenges, but they were better equipped to handle them.

They also recognized the importance of staying flexible and open to new ideas. As their children grew and their needs changed, they were prepared to adapt their strategies accordingly. They were committed to continuous learning and improvement, both for themselves and their children.

Encouraging Other Parents

Sarah and Rachel hoped that their story would inspire other parents of children with ADHD. They wanted to share their message of hope, resilience, and the power of community. Here are some words of encouragement for other parents embarking on a similar journey:

1. You Are Not Alone: Remember that you are not alone in this journey. Seek out other parents, support groups, and professionals who can provide guidance and support. Sharing your experiences and learning from others can make a significant difference.

2. Celebrate Small Victories: Celebrate every small victory, no matter how minor it may seem. These small successes add up over time and contribute to your child's overall progress.

3. Be Patient and Persistent: Patience and persistence are key. Finding the right strategies takes time, and there will be setbacks along the way. Stay committed to your child's growth and keep trying different approaches until you find what works.

4. Stay Informed: Stay informed about ADHD and the latest research and strategies. Knowledge is empowering and can help you make better decisions for your child.

5. Build a Support Network: Surround yourself with supportive people who understand your journey. A strong support network can provide emotional strength, practical advice, and a sense of community.

6. Involve Your Child: Involve your child in the process. Encourage them to express their feelings, set goals, and take responsibility for their actions. Empowering your child to

take an active role in managing their ADHD can lead to greater self-awareness and independence.

Final Thoughts

As Sarah, Rachel, and their families continued their journey, they remained committed to supporting their children with love, patience, and understanding. They knew that the road ahead would have its challenges, but they were confident in their ability to navigate it together. By documenting their journey, creating a supportive environment, and building a strong network, they had laid the foundation for a brighter future for Ethan and Emily.

The strategies and systems they developed were not just about managing ADHD; they were about empowering their children to thrive. With each step forward, they reinforced the message that with the right support, anything is possible.

For other parents embarking on a similar journey, Sarah and Rachel's story is a beacon of hope and a reminder that you are not alone. Together, with resilience and community, you can create a world where your child can reach their full potential and flourish in all aspects of life.

WORKSHEET IDEAS

Parents can use these worksheet examples to provide structured support for their children with ADHD, helping them develop essential skills and maintain a sense of routine and stability. Each worksheet is designed to address specific challenges that children with ADHD often face, such as organization, time management, behavior tracking, and social skills development.

Daily Schedule Worksheet

This worksheet helps parents and children collaboratively create a consistent daily routine. By mapping out activities from morning to bedtime, parents can help their child understand what to expect throughout the day, reducing anxiety and improving focus.

Use this worksheet to help your child create a consistent daily schedule. Include time for school,

homework, chores, and leisure activities.

1. Morning Routine:

2. School Hours:

3. Homework Time:

4. Chore Time:

5. Leisure/Play Time:

6. Evening Routine:

7. Bedtime:

Homework Tracker

This tool assists children in keeping track of their assignments and due dates. Parents can review the tracker with their child daily, ensuring that tasks are completed on time and teaching the importance of accountability.

This worksheet will help your child keep track of their homework assignments and due dates.

Subject: ___________

Assignment: ___________

Due Date: ___________

Completed: Yes / No

Chore Chart

Assigning and tracking household responsibilities can be made easier with this chart. It helps children develop a sense of responsibility and accomplishment as they complete their chores, while also reinforcing the importance of contributing to the family.

Create a chore chart to help your child manage their responsibilities at home.

Chore: __________

Day: __________

Completed: Yes / No

Behavioral Goals Worksheet

This worksheet allows parents and children to set and track specific behavioral goals. By identifying desired behaviors and the steps needed to achieve them, parents can provide consistent encouragement and positive reinforcement.

Set and track behavioral goals for your child.

Behavioral Goal: __________

Why This Goal is Important: __________

Steps to Achieve This Goal: __________

Progress: __________

Positive Reinforcement Chart

Parents can use this chart to reward their child for positive behavior and achievements. By earning points for good behavior, children are motivated to continue making positive choices.

Use this chart to reward your child for positive behavior and achievements.

Behavior: __________

Points Earned: __________

Reward: __________

Date: __________

Weekly Reflection Journal

Encouraging children to reflect on their week helps them develop self-awareness and critical thinking. Parents can discuss these reflections with their child, reinforcing positive behaviors and addressing challenges.

Encourage your child to reflect on their week with this journal worksheet.

1. What went well this week?

2. What challenges did you face?

3. How did you overcome these challenges?

4. What goals do you have for next week?

Mindfulness Activity Worksheet

Encouraging children to reflect on their week helps them develop self-awareness and critical thinking. Parents can discuss these reflections with their child, reinforcing positive behaviors and addressing challenges.

Help your child practice mindfulness with this activity worksheet.

1. Describe a time when you felt calm and focused.

2. What helped you feel this way?

3. Practice a deep breathing exercise and describe how you feel afterwards.

Social Skills Worksheet

Use this worksheet to help your child develop social skills.

1. Describe a recent social interaction that went well.

2. What did you do that helped make it a positive experience?

3. Describe a social interaction that was challenging.

4. What could you do differently next time?

Time Management Worksheet

By integrating these worksheets into daily routines, parents can provide structured, consistent support, helping their children develop essential life skills and manage their ADHD effectively.

Teach your child time management skills with this worksheet.

1. List your tasks for the day:

2. Estimate how long each task will take:

3. Prioritize your tasks:

4. Set a timer for each task:

5. Reflect on what worked and what didn't:

Family Meeting Agenda

Parents can use the Family Meeting Agenda worksheet to create a structured and productive environment for regular family discussions, fostering open communication and collaboration. This tool helps ensure that everyone in the family is heard, important topics are addressed, and collective goals are set and achieved.

Use this worksheet to plan and conduct productive family meetings.

1. Date and Time of Meeting: ___________

2. Topics to Discuss:

3. Goals for the Meeting:

4. Action Items:

5. Next Meeting Date: ___________

MY OWN PATH

My journey has been deeply influenced by personal experiences that have shaped my understanding of compassion, resilience, and the complexities of family dynamics. As I pursue my EdD in Educational Psychology, I reflect on the many challenges I have faced and the lessons I have learned, allowing me to speak from a position of experience rather than purely clinical training. This personal connection enables me to relate to what families are going through because I have gone through it as well.

In my own family, we have navigated a multitude of difficult issues: drug abuse, mental illness, depression, foster care, adoption, blended families, neurodivergent children, and autism. Each of these experiences has taught me valuable lessons about empathy, patience, and the importance of a supportive network. Watching a loved one struggle with addiction brings a unique kind of heartache, testing the limits of patience and compassion and often pushing you to the brink of despair. Through this ordeal, I learned the importance of unconditional love and the necessity of boundaries. Supporting someone in recovery is a delicate balance of being there for them while also protecting your own well-being.

Mental illness has also profoundly impacted my family. These conditions carry a heavy stigma, making it difficult for those affected to seek help. Witnessing the struggles of a family member with a mental illness has taught me to approach these issues with a non-judgmental attitude and a willingness to listen. It reinforced the idea that mental health is as crucial as physical health and that seeking professional help is a sign of strength, not weakness. Depression is another battle we have faced. It is a silent, insidious illness that can sap the joy out of life. Supporting a loved one through depression requires immense patience and understanding. I learned to recognize the signs of depression and the importance of encouraging treatment while providing a stable and loving environment.

The experiences of foster care and adoption introduced me to the complexities of blended families. Bringing children into your home, whether temporarily or permanently, is a profound act of love that comes with its own set of challenges. The emotional baggage that foster children carry can be overwhelming, and creating a sense of security and belonging for them requires dedication and compassion. Adoption, too, is a beautiful but complex process that involves navigating the child's feelings of loss and identity while integrating them into their new family. Raising neurodivergent children and a child with autism has been a journey filled with both challenges and rewards. Understanding that each child is unique and requires individualized support has been crucial. It has taught me to appreciate the diverse ways in which children learn and interact with the world. Advocacy has become second nature to me, as ensuring that my children receive the support they need in educational and social settings is a constant effort.

Professionally, I have worked with children facing trauma, depression, adoption, foster care, family separation, involvement in the legal system, gang culture, poverty, and many other adversities. These experiences have further honed my skills and deepened my empathy. Working with children who have experienced trauma is incredibly challenging yet rewarding. Trauma can manifest in numerous ways, affecting a child's behavior, emotions, and ability to trust. My approach has always been to provide a safe and nurturing environment where children feel heard and valued. Building trust takes time, but it is the cornerstone of helping a child heal from traumatic experiences. Depression in children is particularly heartbreaking. It is often overlooked or misunderstood, leading to a lack of proper support. My professional role involves recognizing the signs of depression early and intervening with appropriate therapeutic strategies. It also means educating families about the importance of mental health care and providing them with the resources they need.

Adoption and foster care are areas where my personal and professional experiences intersect. Understanding the emotional complexities involved in these processes allows me to support children and families more effectively. Whether it’s helping a child navigate their feelings of loss and identity or supporting a foster family through the challenges of integration, my goal is to ensure that every child feels loved and secure. Family separation, often due to legal issues or immigration, is another area I have worked in. The trauma of being separated from a parent or sibling can have long-lasting effects on a child's emotional and psychological well-being. My work involves providing therapeutic support to help these children cope with their feelings of abandonment and loss while advocating for policies that prioritize family unity.

Children in the legal system, whether due to delinquency or custody battles, face significant stress and uncertainty. My role is to provide them with a sense of stability and support during these tumultuous times. This often involves coordinating with legal professionals, social workers, and families to ensure that the child's best interests are always at the forefront. Gang culture and poverty are deeply intertwined issues that affect many of the children I work with. Growing up in impoverished neighborhoods with limited opportunities, these children are often drawn into gang culture as a means of survival and belonging. My approach is to provide them with alternatives through education, mentorship, and community programs that offer hope and a path to a brighter future.

Navigating these personal and professional challenges has significantly shaped my approach to helping families and children. Compassion, resilience, and a deep commitment to making a difference are at the heart of my work. Compassion is not just about feeling for others but actively working to alleviate their suffering. It is about putting yourself in their shoes, understanding their struggles, and offering support without judgment. My experiences have taught me that compassion requires action. Whether it's sitting with a child through their tears, advocating for a family in need, or simply being a reliable presence, every act of kindness matters. Resilience is another critical aspect. Both in my personal life and professional work, I have learned that setbacks are inevitable. What matters is how we respond to them. Building resilience means fostering a positive attitude, learning from failures, and always striving to find solutions.

Through all these experiences, I have developed a profound sense of empathy and a commitment to helping others navigate their own challenges. My pursuit of an EdD in Educational Psychology is driven by a desire to deepen my understanding of these issues and to develop effective strategies for supporting children and families. The lessons I've learned from my personal and professional experiences have given me the tools and insights needed to make a meaningful impact. By sharing my journey and the knowledge I've gained, I hope to inspire others to approach these challenges with compassion and resilience, and to provide the support that every child and family deserves.

THANK YOU

Dear Reader,

Thank you for taking the time to read this book. Your commitment to understanding and supporting children with ADHD is a testament to your dedication and love. Whether you are a parent, caregiver, educator, or professional, your role in the lives of these children is invaluable, and your efforts make a significant difference. This book was born out of both personal and professional experiences. Having navigated the complexities of ADHD and related challenges within my own family, as well as working with children facing trauma, depression, foster care, adoption, family separation, involvement in the legal system, gang culture, and poverty, I understand the multifaceted nature of these issues. My journey has been one of learning, adapting, and growing, and it is from this place of experience that I share these insights with you. The strategies, tools, and stories in this book are designed to provide practical guidance and emotional support. I hope they have offered you new perspectives and actionable steps to help the children in your care.

As you continue on this journey, remember that you are not alone. Many families and professionals face similar challenges, and together, we can create a supportive community. Sharing your experiences, both successes and struggles, can help others and foster a sense of solidarity. It is through collective effort and mutual support that we can make the greatest impact. Parents, your love and support are the foundation upon which your child's growth and development are built. Educators, your influence extends beyond the classroom, and your willingness to adapt teaching methods can make a significant difference in a child's educational journey. Professionals, your expertise and compassion are vital, and your ability to provide evidence-based interventions can change the trajectory of a child's life.

To everyone reading this book, I extend my deepest gratitude. Your willingness to learn and grow is a powerful step towards creating a more understanding and supportive world for children with ADHD. The journey may be challenging, but it is also incredibly rewarding. As you move forward, continue to seek out knowledge and support, stay connected with others who share your experiences, and maintain hope and resilience. Every child has the potential to thrive, and with the right support, they can achieve great things. Thank you once again for reading this book and for your dedication to making a difference. Your efforts are truly appreciated, and I am honored to be a part of your journey. Together, we can create a brighter future for all children.

With gratitude,

Steven Fitch

www.ingramcontent.com/pod-product-compliance
Lightning Source LLC
La Vergne TN
LVHW090530110826
845146LV00003B/1048

* 9 7 9 8 8 9 3 7 9 8 2 7 2 *